The Caterpillar
and the Butterfly

By C. Everett

ISBN:
ISBN-13: 978-0-9994624-2-3

Morning Song Publishing

DEDICATION

To Big Boy and Pee Wee
Who are now living a new adventure

CONTENTS

ACKNOWLEDGMENTS

Stock photos provided by Dreamstime

C. Everett

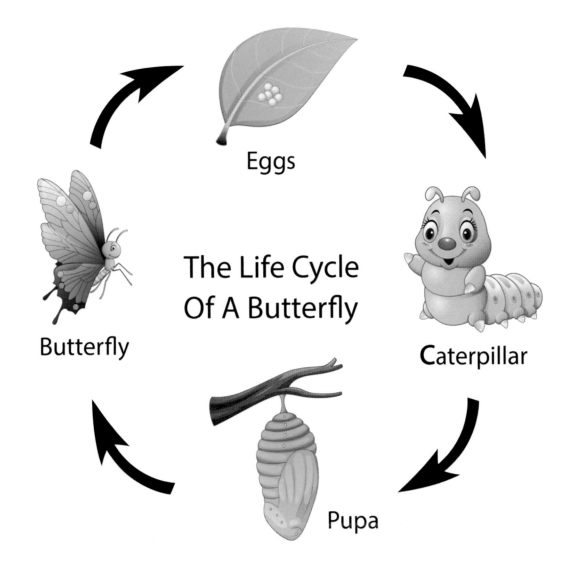

Eggs

Caterpillar

The Life Cycle
Of A Butterfly

Butterfly

Pupa

CHAPTER ONE
SAMMY THE CATERPILLAR

The caterpillars around Sammy busily ate green leaves, seemingly happy and content, while he, on the other hand, looked up with a small frown, his liquid brown eyes sad as he gazed thoughtfully at them.

I wonder why I'm the only one worried about this, he thought to himself. In all the time he could remember, no one had talked about what was to come, though they all, of course, knew that it was inevitable.

Sammy lowered his head back down to the dew-glistened leaf he perched delicately on, willing himself to eat, but he had lost his appetite. Sighing and lost in thought, he started wandering aimlessly from leaf to branch to other leaves, until startled by a rustling above him, he stopped and raised his head as he squinted into the sun.

There, flitting above his head, was a butterfly, his exquisitely arched wings dazzling with the sun that filtered through the colorful patterns.

Sammy scowled. Even though he secretly admired the beautiful creatures, right now they only reminded him of how unimportant he felt.

CHAPTER TWO
SAMMY MEETS A BUTTERFLY

Sammy ignored the butterfly, but it seemed the more he ignored it, the closer it came, until finally in exasperation he spoke.

"Please go away," he sputtered, "can't you go find some flowers or something?"

To Sammy's surprise the butterfly laughed softly at him, then landed on the leaf next to him as though to torment him all the more.

"And leave you to your eating you mean?" the butterfly smiled. "It seems to me that something is eating at *you* instead."

"What would you know about me?" Sammy retorted, scooting back some from the butterfly, all of a sudden noticing just how small the leaf now seemed to be.

"I know, little caterpillar," the butterfly responded, tilting his antennas towards Sammy.

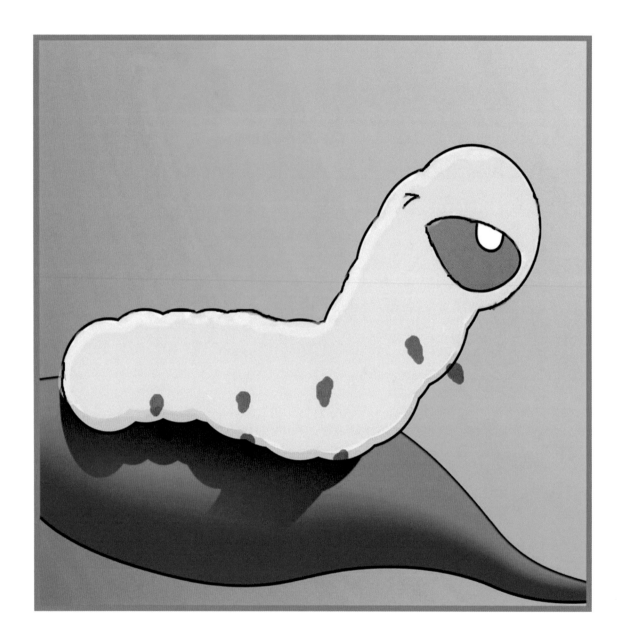

"I've been watching you and I see that you're troubled, and you worry for nothing," he continued.

"That's easy for you to say," Sammy replied sulkily.

The butterfly glanced side-long at Sammy, then flew backwards suddenly, acrobating through the air before landing again close to the caterpillar.

"Now, what's so bad about being able to do that?" he asked still smiling.

Sammy's face fell, "I don't want to change," he whispered, "why must I? It's not fair! I want to be me. Let the others become butterflies if they want, but I *like* being a caterpillar."

The butterfly rested his wing on Sammy briefly in a friendly pat, "You once were an egg. Do you wish that you had stayed one?"

"Of course not," Sammy replied in a huff.

"Then what is it that you are really fighting?"

"Because," Sammy spoke intently, "the others tell me I don't even have a choice. I have to stop being a caterpillar, even if I don't want to."

"Ah," said the butterfly, "you want to choose. And would you ever choose on your own to become a butterfly, my lad? It's quite a wondrous thing you know."

Sammy scrunched his small face in thought, dwelling on what the butterfly said, when suddenly the butterfly flapped his wings and rose into the air shaking his head at Sammy in amusement.

"I'll visit again tomorrow, if you like."

And with that, and a chuckle, the butterfly fluttered away.

CHAPTER THREE
SAMMY AND WILLOW

That night Sammy rested. His thoughts drifted back to the butterfly he met earlier, before finally falling into sleep and strange dreams in which he could fly.

In the morning he arose with the dawning of the sun and joined the others as they gathered, soon to go in search of breakfast leaves.

Sammy's best friend was Willow, who now approached him with smile, traced with a tinge of worry. "Hi Sammy," she greeted brightly.

"Hi back, Willow." Sammy returned her smile, knowing that Willow must have wondered why he had been so glum lately. Grinning he pushed her playfully with his head until she laughed, a tinkling, lilting sound that never failed to make him feel happier.

The two friends walked together towards the nearest tree branch, as they did most mornings, only this morning Willow thought that Sammy seemed even more quiet than he had the last few days.

"Is everything okay Sammy?" she asked.

Sammy gave a small smile to his friend and nodded, "I'm sorry I have been so quiet Willow, I've just been thinking about things lately."

"Thinking about what?" Willow asked.

"Well, don't you ever think that maybe you would like to stay a caterpillar?" he asked.

Willow gave Sammy a baffled look. "Why ever would I want that? Especially when the next thing we'll be are pretty butterflies!"

"Yes, but…how do you know that you'll like it?" Sammy asked. "I mean, you know that you like being a caterpillar, but what will you do if you become a butterfly and wish you were a caterpillar again?"

Willow giggled at him, "Do we have a choice Sammy?"

"I guess not," Sammy muttered, "still, I can't help but wonder."

"Well, we can't stay caterpillars, and I'll be glad to be a butterfly and have wings. It's a wonderful adventure!" Willow spun around happily as she grinned at her friend.

Sammy smiled back, and soon the two caterpillars were eating their breakfast in earnest, talk of butterflies all but forgotten.

CHAPTER FOUR
RETURN OF THE BUTTERFLY

After a while, Sammy noticed the same butterfly from yesterday sitting quietly on a leaf and waving his antennas right at him. Excusing himself, he slowly approached the butterfly, cocking his head slightly as he neared.

"Hello again little one," the butterfly greeted warmly.

"Hello again butterfly," Sammy replied a little shyly, but warily as well. "Are you waiting for me?" he asked.

The butterfly nodded, the tips of his wings tilting lightly in the breeze.

"But why?" asked Sammy, "Why me?"

"Did you want me to come?" smiled the butterfly.

"Well, yes, I suppose I did," Sammy answered.

"Then that's why I came," the butterfly nodded with a little chuckle.

Sammy nodded back at the butterfly, then not knowing what else to do, began to nibble slowly at the leaf, watching the butterfly out of the corner of his eye. They both were quiet for a while, then the butterfly gently broke the silence.

"I must admit that I find this all very intriguing," he mused, "Why fret so, really?"

Sammy stopped nibbling and thought for a minute before responding.

"I am a caterpillar, and I don't understand why that isn't enough."

"I'm told I have to become a butterfly like you. But, if I become a butterfly, then I won't be me anymore, I won't be Sammy the Caterpillar. I'll be…well, I'm not sure who I'll be really," he said, a flicker of sadness shining from his eyes as he looked up at the butterfly.

"Little caterpillar," the butterfly clucked, "the butterfly is already inside you. Tell me," he continued, "do you really never dream in your heart of hearts of flying?"

CHAPTER FIVE
SAMMY RECONSIDERS

Sammy blushed at the question, not wanting to answer, but the butterfly saw the truth in his face. "Well, that's not the point though," he responded stubbornly. "What's so much better about being a butterfly?"

"It's not better, little one, it's different," the butterfly replied patiently.

"I won't still be me," Sammy whispered.

The butterfly laughed, "You won't be what you are right now, you will be something more. As today you are something more than you were yesterday."

"I like things the way they are now," Sammy said thoughtfully. "I think I would like very much if they didn't change."

The butterfly patted Sammy with the tip of his wing, looking amused before finally speaking.

"Just think, little caterpillar, if there were no changes then you would always be thinking the same thought, standing in the same place, feeling the same feeling. You would be frozen in time."

"In fact," he continued, "with no change there wouldn't even be any time. The only way that you will stop being you is if nothing ever changed."

He looked at Sammy with a twinkle in his eye. "And with that, my little friend," he laughed, "I must take my leave."

"I wish you well on your journey and please remember to live your adventure, for truly it will be one like no other."

The butterfly gazed fondly at Sammy as he readied himself to leave.

"Wait, please," Sammy asked with a sheepish smile. "I don't even know your name."

"You may call me what you like," the butterfly smiled in reply.

"Well," said Sammy, "then what is it that you call yourself?"

The butterfly laughed. "I call myself Me."

"Well, that's silly," grinned Sammy, "because that's what I call myself too!"

They both chuckled together before the butterfly flew away, then Sammy went to go and look for Willow, still smiling to himself and feeling very much now like living a new adventure.

CHAPTER SIX
LIVING THE ADVENTURE

The sun seemed to sparkle as it rose on a new day, the warming rays glinting off of the dew - covered leaves. The forest slowly came alive as the dawn broke, stirring the creatures as the birds began to sing their songs to the morning.

The multi-colored butterfly circled above the tree, coming closer and closer to the little caterpillar before alighting on a leaf not too far from him.

The caterpillar, who seemed lost in thought, glanced up in surprise at the butterfly, and almost immediately frowned.

"What are you doing here butterfly?" he asked.

The butterfly smiled knowingly at the caterpillar, then flitted his wings happily as if he found much pleasure in the feel of them.

"I was just visiting," he said. "I've noticed you here in this same spot most mornings, but you don't seem to be enjoying your breakfast very much." The butterfly pointed his antennas to the barely eaten leaf to emphasize his point.

The caterpillar sighed. "I've just been thinking about things lately is all," he replied. "What is your name butterfly?"

"Well," smiled the butterfly, "I call myself Me, but if you like you may call me Sammy."

Sammy's wings quivered as he took flight, lazily circling above the caterpillars' head, before expertly landing next to him. "So, little caterpillar," he said with a contagious smile, "maybe we could chat for a little while."

The End and….
The Beginning

C. Everett

ABOUT THE AUTHOR

C. Everett grew up in Florida, well familiar with the colorful and once plentiful caterpillar. She has a particular fondness for the caterpillars, the plump and fuzzy bumblebee, the friendly and delicate ladybug, and the little mentioned, but equally fascinating, dragonfly. Please look for more of these stories to come, and enjoy!

C. Everett

Made in the USA
Coppell, TX
01 October 2021